What's-Up Dumplings
→ Page 50

"Cheeseburger" Dumplings
→ Page 52

Contents

Beech Mushroom & Pork Dumplings
→ Page 54

Garlic Scape Dumplings with Beef
→ Page 56

Pork Dumplings with Shiso
→ Page 58

Gyoza Bolognese with Fresh Tomato
→ Page 60

Tofu Dumplings with Okra & Pickled Ginger
→ Page 62

T0020744

Dancing Octopus Dumplings
→ Page 66

(22)

Kelp & Clam Gyoza
→ Page 68

(23) **Bell Pepper Dumplings with Egg**
→ Page 70

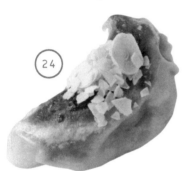

(24)

(25) **Simmered Pork Belly Dumplings**
→ Page 74

(26)

The "Colonel's" Crispy Chicken Dumplings
→ Page 76

Shiitake & Pork Potstickers
→ Page 72

(29) **Corned Beef & Shallot Pot-stickers**
→ Page 82

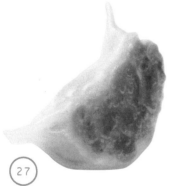

(27)

Radish & Shredded Squid Dumplings
→ Page 78

(28)

Crunchy Land Seaweed Gyoza
→ Page 80

(30) **Sweet Potato Dumplings**
→ Page 84

31
Buttery Abalone Gyoza
→ Page 86

32
Angelic Ashitaba Dumplings
→ Page 88

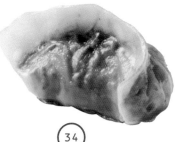

33
Okra & Nameko Mushroom Gyoza
→ Page 90

34
Squid Ink, Konnyaku & Anchovy Gyoza
→ Page 92

35
Lotus Root & Pork Belly Potstickers
→ Page 94

36
Sweet Eel Dumplings
→ Page 96

37
Cheesy Chikuwa Gyoza
→ Page 98

38
Pollock Roe & Prawn Potstickers
→ Page 100

39
Snappy Tuna Potstickers
→ Page 102

40
Cherry Blossom Dumplings
→ Page 104

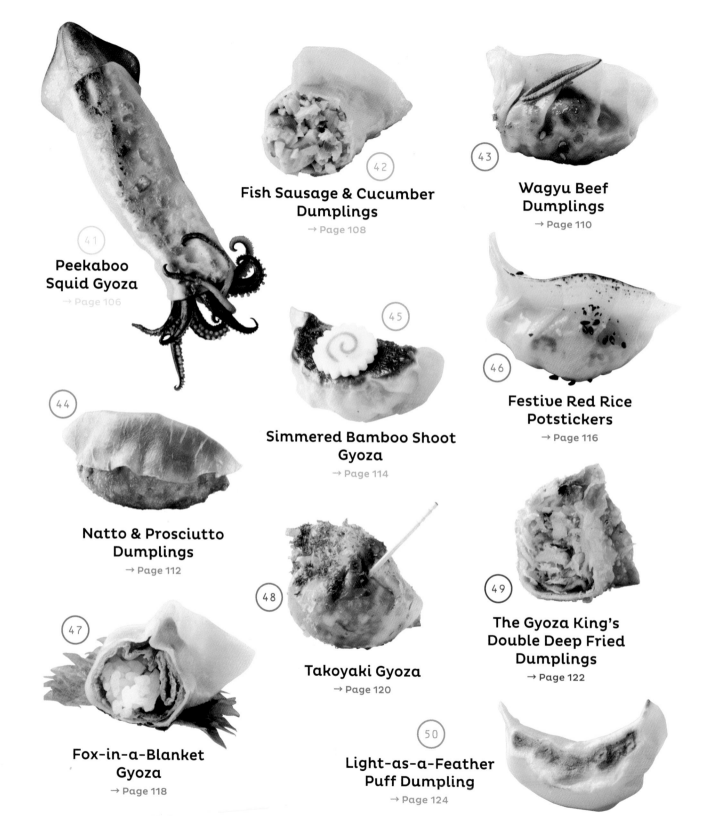

Peekaboo Squid Gyoza
→ Page 106

Fish Sausage & Cucumber Dumplings
→ Page 108

Wagyu Beef Dumplings
→ Page 110

Natto & Prosciutto Dumplings
→ Page 112

Simmered Bamboo Shoot Gyoza
→ Page 114

Festive Red Rice Potstickers
→ Page 116

Fox-in-a-Blanket Gyoza
→ Page 118

Takoyaki Gyoza
→ Page 120

The Gyoza King's Double Deep Fried Dumplings
→ Page 122

Light-as-a-Feather Puff Dumpling
→ Page 124

GYOZA

The Ultimate Dumpling Cookbook

Vine Garden Friends
—Let's Eat!

TUTTLE Publishing

Tokyo | Rutland, Vermont | Singapore

Introduction

Humans have almost certainly been eating dumplings for about a long as they have been cultivating cabbages and wheat—or at least since the switchover from BC to AD!

The personal mission of Paradise Yamamoto—popularly known as Japan's "Gyoza King"—is to spread the gospel of dumplings as far and wide as he possibly can. At his members-only "Vine Garden" pop-up dinners in Tokyo he serves only dumplings and wraps each one with love.

This book is his first effort to teach home cooks all of his secrets and share the joys of making great dumplings at home through 50 easy-to-follow recipes.

Here you'll find traditional dumplings alongside Yamamoto's own outlandishly new and creative ones. His desire is to expand your horizons so that in 10 years dumplings containing Parmesan cheese and prosciutto or octopus and fish roe will be as common as the usual ones filled with cabbage, leeks and pork.

Please give all of his dumplings a try! You too may become a dumpling disciple!

Foreword

Every cuisine has a dumpling to showcase. Morsels of mostly savory ingredients are stuffed into pockets of pliable dough, then pinched, pleated or folded into bite-sized surprise packages. Eastern European *kreplach*, Turkish *manti*, Chinese *jiaozi*, and Japanese *gyoza* share delicious DNA.

Now the improbably named Paradise Yamamoto has added even more variety to this widely loved but commonplace treat. This industrial designer, musician and certified Santa Claus has beaten as eclectic a path to the dumpling as his name suggests, and is today surely the most creative wrapper of uniquely filled gyoza south of the North Pole. We met at a café in Tokyo and I asked how he got his name. Wearing his signature knitted beanie, he told me he wants to feel and spread happiness every day.

I have been eating and making gyoza since I first came to Japan forty-five years ago as a young bride. Through decades of practice I became proficient in pleating the delicious pork and cabbage crescent. But Yamamoto-san's kaleidoscope of possibilities inspired me—and many of his Japanese readers—to break the bonds of convention. The

array of mouth-watering dumpling photos you see on this book's cover prompted one Japanese friend to exclaim "*yatte mitai*" (I want to try making this)!

Yamamoto-san insists that we not use preground pork. "Chop your own," he admonished me. I did, and was astonished by the difference it made in the perfectly seasoned pork and mushroom gyoza I laid before grateful diners. A game of rock, paper, scissors determined who got the last dumpling! He also counsels us not to use the standard trinity of soy sauce, vinegar and chili oil for dipping. A sprinkling of salt allows the flavors to shine through. Revelatory!

He is as thoughtful about his implements as his ingredients. His pan of choice is "the cheapest frying pan I can find," because the thin layer of metal does a great job browning and crisping. He buys as many as he can when he sees them on sale, and may splurge by adding a glass lid that, while still inexpensive, may cost more than the pan.

In this book he uses store-bought wrappers so readers can concentrate on the fillings. And, oh, what fillings! You will be enchanted by his formulas for mixing meat and vegetables, by his combinations like broccoli and eggs that appeal to kids' palates, and by an Italian-inspired carbonara dumpling with bacon, egg whites and Parmesan cheese that prompted a restaurateur of a hip Brooklyn eatery to declare, "These would be huge on a New York brunch menu."

This book challenges, delights, and inspires. Yamamoto-san told me that serving people what you have made by your own hand provides love and sustenance, and is an act of intimacy. But don't forget the whimsy as well—whether producing savory courses or sweet dessert dumplings, you can practice your culinary origami as you twist, crimp and fold the skins around the fillings to form penguins, sailor hats, and Santa's toy sacks. Talk about spreading happiness—Ho! Ho! Ho!

—Debra Samuels

Garlic Chives (*Nira*)

These flat, mildly aromatic leaves are a gyoza staple. An Asian market with a decent produce section should have them. If you can't find them, you can substitute an equal quantity of chopped round chives or green onion (scallion) greens, plus a little crushed fresh garlic.

Celery

Celery adds freshness and crunch to your filling. Cut a stick of celery lengthwise into strips before cutting crosswise for a fine dice. Use the leaves, too!

The Gyoza Pantry

Ten basic ingredients to make your dumplings

Ginger Root

An essential addition, fresh ginger will give your gyoza a bit of heat and liveliness. Look for firm, unwrinkled roots with smooth brown skin. Peel before chopping, grating, or grinding. Extra ginger root can be frozen whole.

Pork Belly

This is the secret to making juicy, richly flavored gyoza. Thinly sliced pork belly (sold as "uncured bacon" in the US) is easiest to chop up.

Cabbage

Use common green cabbage; it should be easy to find. Remove the tough bottom part of the central vein before chopping individual leaves finely. Napa cabbage or bok choy leaves can be used in a pinch, but be aware that they may contain more moisture than green cabbage.

Pork Loin

Pork is the traditional meat of choice for gyoza. You'll be amazed at the difference in flavor and texture when you mince it yourself instead of buying ground meat. Boneless pork loin is easiest to manage, and its leanness is balanced out with an equal quantity of chopped pork belly.

Shaoxing Rice Wine

This rice wine, from a specific region of China, is aged to take on the characteristics of dry sherry. It is widely available in Asian markets. Dry sherry or sake may be substituted if you can't find Shaoxing wine.

Green Onions (Scallions)

If you can find long, slender Japanese leeks (called *naganegi*) in your local Asian market, they are preferable. Otherwise, conventional green onions are fine. Trim away the roots and any wilted leaves, and use both the green and white parts.

Shiitake Mushrooms

Fresh shiitakes are becoming more widely available. You can find them in well-stocked produce sections, as well as at some farmers' markets. Dried shiitakes, which are also easy to obtain, have a richer flavor than fresh. To reconstitute dried mushrooms, place in a bowl of filtered water, weight with a small plate, and let stand in a cool place or the refrigerator for 8 hours or overnight. Drain and reserve the soaking water for another purpose, like soup stock. If you're in a hurry, you can reconstitute them in 30 minutes with boiling water, but the flavor and texture are better with a slow soak.

Gyoza Wrappers

Egg roll wrappers, wonton wrappers, dumpling skins . . . these thin sheets of wheat-flour dough go by many names. They are available in a range of shapes, sizes, and quantities at both conventional and Asian markets. For the recipes in this book, look for gyoza wrappers, which are about 3½ inches (9 cm) in diameter and come in packages of about fifty. You may be able to find larger wrappers, about 4 inches (10 cm) in diameter; these are preferable for certain recipes. If you can only find square-shaped wrappers, worry not! You can use a pastry cutter or other appropriately sized round object (tin can, drinking glass, etc.) to cut them into circles.

Garlic Chives

1 Chop finely into ⅛ to ¼-inch (4 to 6-mm) pieces.

2

3

Shiitake Mushrooms

1 Dice as thoroughly as you can.

2 It will take effort ...

3 ... to get it this fine.

Celery

1

2 Use the leaves too!

Scallions

1 Cut both the green and white parts.

2

Chopping Methods

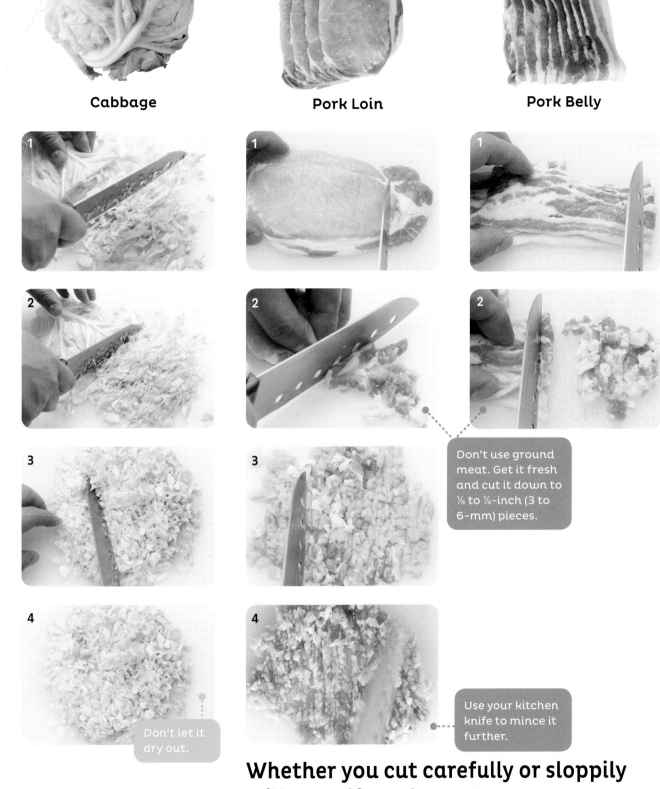

Cabbage

Pork Loin

Pork Belly

Don't use ground meat. Get it fresh and cut it down to ⅛ to ¼-inch (3 to 6-mm) pieces.

Don't let it dry out.

Use your kitchen knife to mince it further.

Whether you cut carefully or sloppily will not affect the taste.

Meat & Vegetable Filling

[For 25 Pieces]
(about 2 cups / 400 g total)
Preparation time: 30 minutes
Use about 2 teaspoons of the meat-vegetable mix in each dumpling.

Mix 1 cup (200 g) of the Chopped Meat Filling (see opposite) with:
½ cup (25 g) chopped green onions (scallions)
⅓ cup (25 g) chopped garlic chives
¼ cup (25 g) chopped celery
½ teaspoon salt
½ cup (50 g) finely chopped green cabbage
2 shiitake mushrooms, reconstituted if dried, chopped fine

Add the meat, then mix in the vegetables. The ratio should be about 1:1.

Preparing Your Fillings

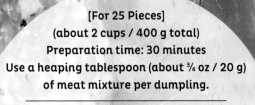

[For 25 Pieces]
(about 2 cups / 400 g total)
Preparation time: 30 minutes
Use a heaping tablespoon (about ¾ oz / 20 g)
of meat mixture per dumpling.

---

6 oz (175 g) pork belly, finely chopped
6 oz (175 g) pork loin, minced to ⅛ to ¼ inch (3–6 mm)
2 teaspoons grated ginger
1 teaspoon sugar
1 teaspoon salt
1 teaspoon chicken broth
1 teaspoon coarse black pepper
1 tablespoon sesame oil
1 tablespoon Shaoxing rice wine
or sake

Chopped Meat Filling

Basic Gyoza Dipping Sauce

While just a sprinkling of salt allows the gyoza's flavor to shine brightest, dipping sauce options are infinite. A good traditional sauce is composed of soy sauce, rice vinegar and sesame oil, plus other optional ingredients.

    4 tablespoons soy sauce
    4 tablespoons rice vinegar
    1 teaspoon sesame oil
    ⅛ teaspoon hot chili oil (optional)
    1 teaspoon crushed garlic (optional)
    1 teaspoon grated ginger (optional)
    1 green onion (scallion), green and white parts, thinly sliced (optional)

Combine all ingredients and mix to combine. Let stand for 10 minutes before using. Without optional ingredients, will keep indefinitely. With optional ingredients, refrigerate and use within a week.

Seven Simple Wrapping Methods

I want you to try all
seven of these techniques!

The Crescent

Use your index finger to keep ingredients inside while you begin the fold.

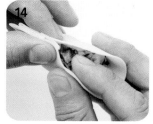

Pinch one end shut and begin to create pleats on one side of the wrapper. Make the folds as even as possible, handling the wrapper gently until all pleats are made.

1

Moisten the edges of the wrapper with water so the two sides stick together.

Push the ingredients deeper inside with your index finger as needed as you make evenly spaced pleats.

2

11

This is the most common wrapping method. The key to the crescent is to layer each fold carefully before pinching tightly closed.

3

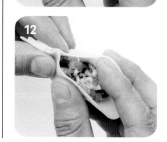

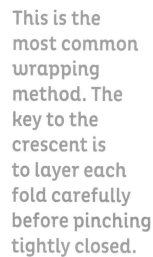

16

17

18

19

20

21
Carefully pinch the overlapping folds to the other side of the wrapper.

22

23
Press the two sides together firmly so that the dumpling is sealed shut.

24

25

26

27

28

29

30

31
A gentle pinch and it's done!

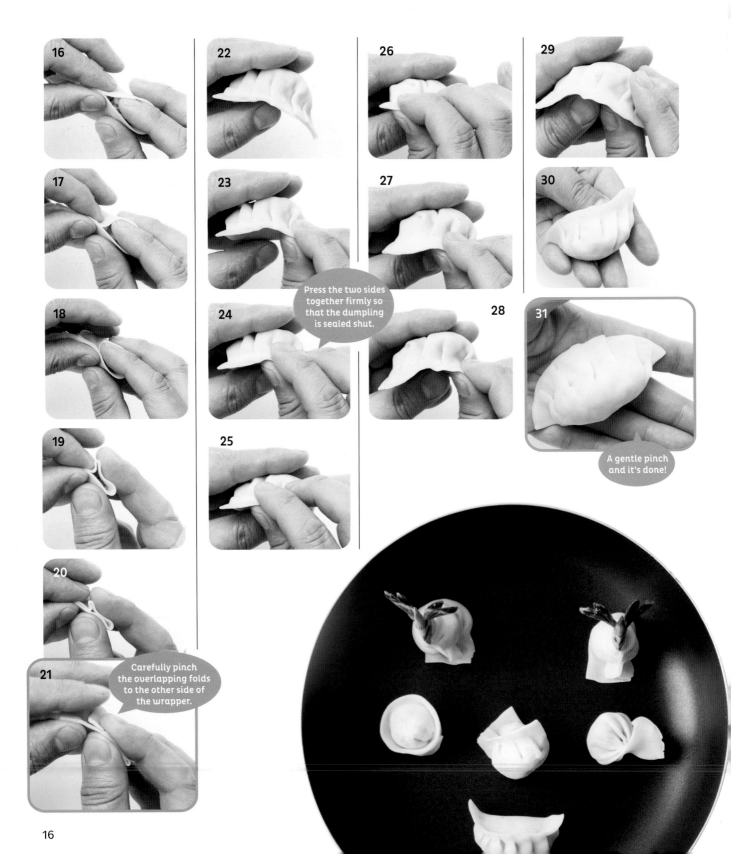

Santa's Gift Bag

This is a newer method, and it can be a little tricky. Practice makes perfect!

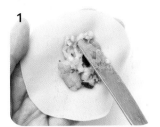

1

2

3

4

5

Make lots and lots of small folds, stacking them on top of each other and holding them firmly between thumb and forefinger.

6

7

8

After you make the final fold, closing the pouch, smash the layers together until they are as thin as a single wrapper.

9

10

11

12

Fold the edge and give it a half-twist.

13

14

15

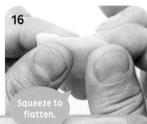

16

Squeeze to flatten.

17

18

The Sailor Cap

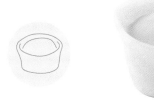

The Russian Navy introduced sailor caps to the world. The sailor cap shape is a fun wrapping technique.

1

2

3

Moisten the edges of the wrapper and fold in half over the filling so that the edges are perfectly aligned. Press firmly to seal the edges together.

4

5

6

This technique does not have any pleats.

7

8

9

10

11

Using your thumb, crease the center.

12

13

14

Pinch the two ends together, using additional water as needed, and press to make an even edge.

15

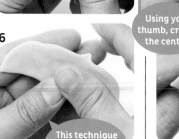

16

17

18

The Volcano

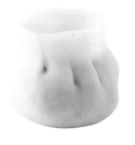

With one of my special fillings, these cute dumplings will "erupt" with flavor!

This is similar to the Seashell wrap, but make five pleats instead of three.

1

2

3

4

5

6

7

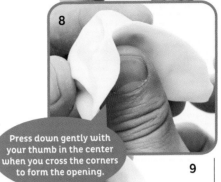

8

Press down gently with your thumb in the center when you cross the corners to form the opening.

9

10

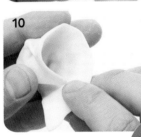

11

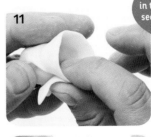

12

13

Align the top edges as you overlap the corners. Pinch to form a high rim of even thickness.

14

15

16

Push your thumb in to keep ingredients securely inside while you finish.

17

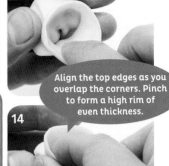

18

The Seashell

This shape is interesting, which helps to highlight something special inside.

7

8

13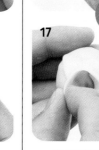

14 Cross the corners so that the top edges line up. Moisten the surfaces with water to aid in sticking if needed.

9

Press the sealed edges firmly to keep the dumpling from opening.

15

Squeeze the layers together until they are as thin as one sheet.

16

Shape the opening with your index finger.

Moisten the edges of the wrapper so it will stick together.

Make two more deep folds and then seal the outside edges together.

1

4

10

Pinch one end together and make a deep fold in one side of the wrapper.

2

5

11

17

Now crush the layers to the thickness of one sheet.

Pull the corners together.

3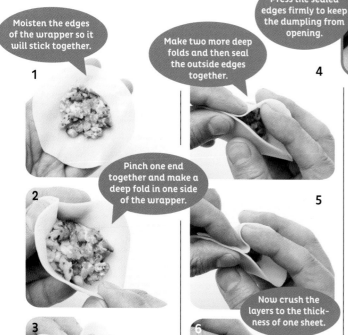

6

12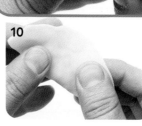

18

The Penguin

This is a variation on the Crescent wrap. The Penguin stands
upright.

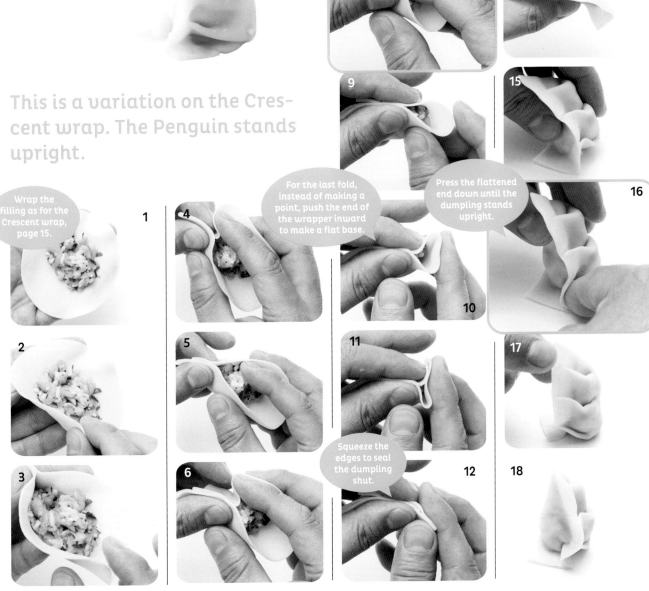

Wrap the
filling as for the
Crescent wrap,
page 15.

1

2

3

4

5

6

For the last fold,
instead of making a
point, push the end of
the wrapper inward
to make a flat base.

Use your index
finger to keep
ingredients inside
while you fold.

7

8

9

10

11

Squeeze the
edges to seal
the dumpling
shut.

12

13

14

15

Press the flattened
end down until the
dumpling stands
upright.

16

17

18

The Handstand

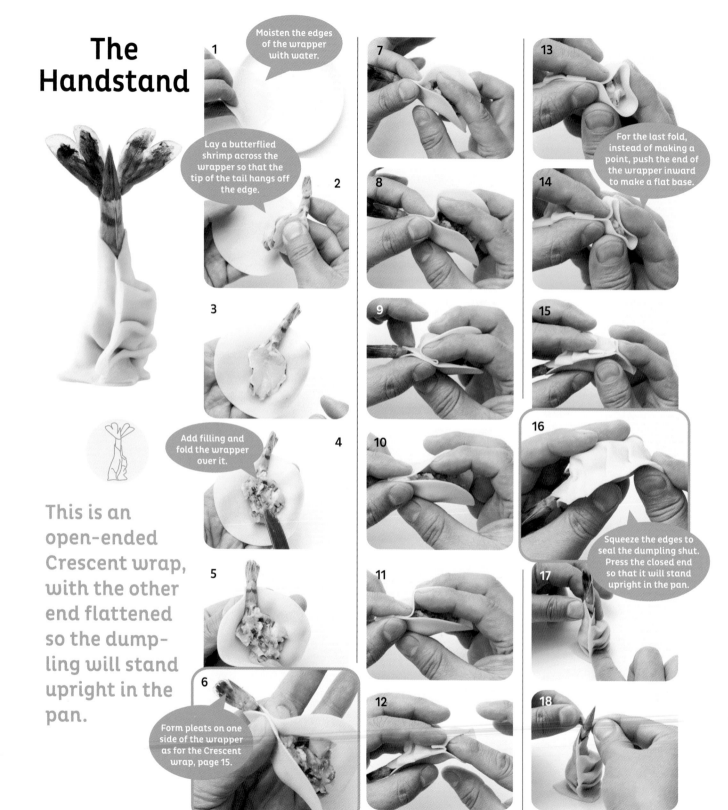

1 Moisten the edges of the wrapper with water.

Lay a butterflied shrimp across the wrapper so that the tip of the tail hangs off the edge.

2

3

4 Add filling and fold the wrapper over it.

5

6 Form pleats on one side of the wrapper as for the Crescent wrap, page 15.

This is an open-ended Crescent wrap, with the other end flattened so the dumpling will stand upright in the pan.

7

8

9

10

11

12

13 For the last fold, instead of making a point, push the end of the wrapper inward to make a flat base.

14

15

16 Squeeze the edges to seal the dumpling shut. Press the closed end so that it will stand upright in the pan.

17

18

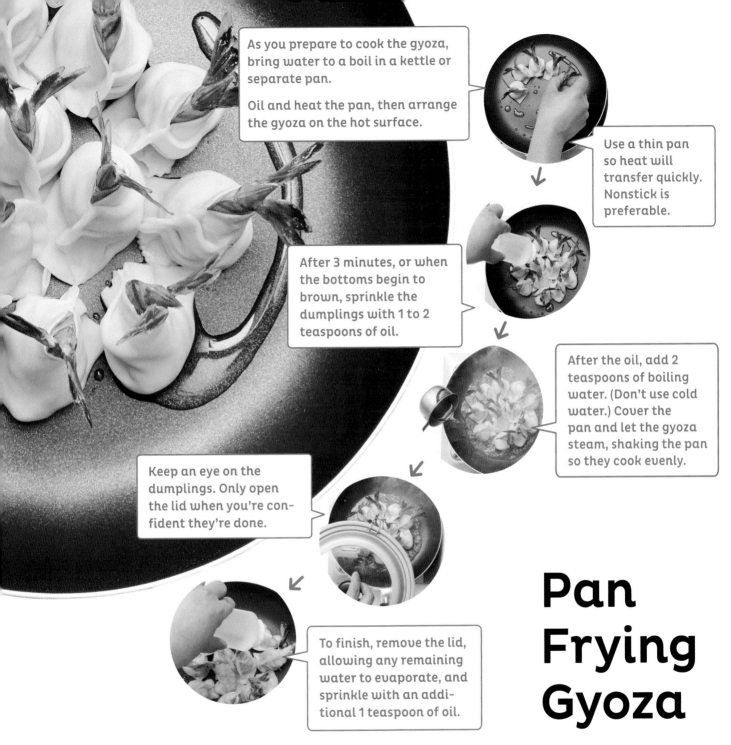

As you prepare to cook the gyoza, bring water to a boil in a kettle or separate pan.

Oil and heat the pan, then arrange the gyoza on the hot surface.

Use a thin pan so heat will transfer quickly. Nonstick is preferable.

After 3 minutes, or when the bottoms begin to brown, sprinkle the dumplings with 1 to 2 teaspoons of oil.

After the oil, add 2 teaspoons of boiling water. (Don't use cold water.) Cover the pan and let the gyoza steam, shaking the pan so they cook evenly.

Keep an eye on the dumplings. Only open the lid when you're confident they're done.

To finish, remove the lid, allowing any remaining water to evaporate, and sprinkle with an additional 1 teaspoon of oil.

Pan Frying Gyoza

Use a high-heat frying oil. Peanut oil, grape seed oil or vegetable oil are all good options. Sesame oil will add a unique depth of flavor.

To form the "blossom" shown below, cluster the gyoza tightly in the pan. Sprinkle with oil. Once you add oil to the dumplings, the sound will change.

After the oil, add 2 teaspoons of boiling water. (Never use cold water, unless you want to create a delicate connective crust, as shown on page 49. To do this, add cold water with ½ teaspoon of *kyorikiko* flour stirred in.)

"Flower Blossom" Pan Frying

You can fuse all the dumplings into a single impressive tear-apart piece.

Cover the pan and let the gyoza steam, shaking the pan so they cook evenly.

To finish, remove the lid and add oil once again.

Once they're cooked, transfer the gyoza to a warm plate and keep them uncovered so they don't get soggy. Serve as soon as possible.

Other Cooking Techniques

Deep Frying: In a heavy pot or deep frying pan, heat 4 inches (10 cm) of oil to 375°F (190°C). Use a slotted spoon or spider skimmer to carefully lower the gyoza into the hot oil. Cook, turning twice, until golden brown (3 to 4 minutes).

Simmering: Bring 4 cups stock or broth to a boil, then lower the heat to medium. Add gyoza one at a time and allow the liquid to return to a boil. Lower the heat. Cover and simmer until just cooked, 2–4 minutes depending on the filling.

Steaming: Prepare a pot with a steamer basket over—not in—boiling water. Place gyoza in the basket and steam until cooked through, 5 to 7 minutes.

Broiling: Cover a cookie sheet with a layer of oven-safe parchment and arrange the gyoza on top. Broil on high for 8 to 10 minutes, checking frequently. If the edges start to brown too fast, lower the rack a little.

The Recipes

Mamgyoen
(Vine Garden
Restaurant)

50 Ways to Make Dumplings

For details on how to make the fillings of each dumpling, see the recipes for Chopped Meat Filling and Meat & Vegetable Filling on pages 12–13.

Place about 2 teaspoons of filling atop each prawn, then wrap.
Fry immediately so the tails don't soften and collapse.

Topsy-Turvy Prawn Potstickers

These prawn potstickers will make waves at your next cocktail party. They can be a little tricky to wrap, though, so use a dab of water to make sure the edges seal properly. You can also dust the center of the wrapper with cornstarch to help keep it from collapsing. Garnish with scallions, water chestnuts or cilantro. Just be sure to set out a discard plate for the uneaten tails!

Serves
10

Prep Time
45 minutes, plus time to make the Meat & Vegetable Filling

Wrapping Method

The Handstand
→ Page 22

Cooking Method
Pan Frying
→ Page 23

MATERIALS
[makes 20]

20 gyoza wrappers (use large size if available)
21 prawns, shelled with tails on, butterflied
¾ cup (150 g) Meat & Vegetable Filling (page 12)
½ avocado, chopped and mixed in with the filling
Chopped water chestnuts, scallions or cilantro (for garnish)

Use a tablespoon of cooked egg for each dumpling. The broccoli and eggs are lightly cooked before wrapping. They'll be perfectly done when the dumplings are golden-brown on the bottom.

Broccoli & Egg Umbrella Dumplings

These fun dumplings are a colorful, enticing way to get the kids (and grownups) to eat their vegetables! The broccoli "umbrellas" give the dumplings some shade, so they cook separately from the egg filling. Scrambled eggs and broccoli go well together, particularly when dipped in soy sauce. For a dipping sauce with a little more kick, mix 1 part soy sauce with 1 part rice vinegar and 1 part toasted sesame oil.

Serves
4

Prep Time
40 minutes

Wrapping Method

The Volcano
→ Page 19

Cooking Method
Pan Frying
→ Page 23

MATERIALS
[makes 8]

---

8 gyoza wrappers (use large size if available)
Eight 3-inch (7-cm) stalks broccoli, lightly steamed or blanched
2 eggs, beaten and cooked just enough to hold together

Crispy Pork Gyoza

A more classic gyoza recipe, these pork dumplings contain a spritz of lime to liven them up! Once the dumplings are wrapped, they can be frozen in an airtight container for up to a week before frying. Between the buttery crunch of fried dough and the succulent taste of Paradise Yamamoto's minced-meat mix, the only risk is not making enough!

Serves
4

Prep Time
40 minutes

Wrapping Method

The Crescent
→ Page 15

Cooking Method
Deep Frying
→ Page 24

MATERIALS
[makes 8]

8 gyoza wrappers (use large size if available)
¾ cup (150 g) Chopped Meat Filling (page 13)
1 or 2 sprigs basil, for garnish
2 (or more) lime wedges, for spritzing

The trick to that beautiful golden-brown color is to fry it twice!

TIP!

Heat the oil to 375°F (190°C). Add the dumplings and fry until they turn light brown. Remove, allow the oil to return to temperature and fry them again until they are a medium golden-brown.

To hard-cook quail eggs, add 4 inches (10 cm) of water to a pan and bring to a boil. Use a slotted spoon to carefully place the quail eggs into the boiling water, then lower heat and boil gently for 3 minutes. Transfer immediately to a cold-water bath and cool fully before peeling.

Use only about 2 teaspoons of curry in each dumpling, and be sure to seal the wrapper firmly so it won't leak!

Curry Potstickers with Quail Eggs

Keema Curry—ground beef with vegetables in a rich curry sauce—arrived in Japan in the '50s and quickly became popular—it's healthy, savory, and easy to make. Use the recipe in the sidebar or follow instructions on a box of Japanese curry roux to make Keema Curry as a main course with rice. Just set some aside for these dumplings.

I like to serve these dumplings alongside *fukujinzuke*, a pickled vegetable mixture with a soy-sauce base. This condiment is available at Japanese markets as well as online, but if you can't find it, a sweet chutney like Major Grey's is a fine complement.

MATERIALS
[makes 8]

8 gyoza wrappers (use large size if available)
3 tablespoons Keema Curry (see below)
2 tablespoons shredded mild cheddar or jack cheese
8 hard-cooked quail eggs (If you can't find quail eggs, hard-boil
2 chicken eggs and put a quarter of an egg in each dumpling)
Fukujinzuke or sweet chutney, as condiment

Serves
4

Prep Time
35 minutes, plus time to make the curry

Wrapping Method

The Volcano
→ Page 19

Cooking Method
Pan Frying
→ Page 23

Keema Curry (makes 4 servings as a main dish. Prep time: 30 minutes)

2 tablespoons cooking oil
1 onion, diced
1 clove garlic, chopped
1 in (2.5 cm) length ginger, chopped finely
2 carrots, diced
1 lb (500 g) ground beef
¼ cup (40 g) frozen peas
¼ cup (40 g) frozen corn
½ cup (125 ml) water
½ box Japanese curry roux (look for Golden Curry or Vermont House brands)
Salt and pepper, to taste

Heat the oil in a large heavy-bottomed saucepan over medium-high heat. Add the onion and sauté until translucent, then add the garlic and the ginger. When the edges of the onion begin to brown, add the carrot and sauté for two minutes more. Stir in the ground beef and cook, breaking up with a wooden spoon, until the meat is no longer red. Add the frozen peas and corn and cook another 3 to 4 minutes, or until heated through. Add the water and stir to combine. Add the cubes of curry roux. Reduce heat to medium-low and continue to cook, stirring, until the cubes are dissolved and the gravy is bubbling. Add a little more water to prevent sticking if needed; season to taste. Serve over hot rice.

TIP!
Be sure to heat oil in the frying pan BEFORE adding the dumplings!

Add half the cumin seeds to the filling, and toss the rest in the pan to fry alongside the dumplings for added flavor.

05

Lamb Gyoza with Coriander

A few hundred years after the fall of Babylon, the upper classes in Baghdad began to really test the limits of lamb in fine dining. One of the major contributions to come from these experiments was the addition of coriander to impart a nutty, citrusy flavor to a succulent rack of lamb. The layer of dough wrapped around these bite-sized morsels softens the spice and rounds out the dish, creating a perfect treat for chilly evenings.

Serves
6

Prep Time
25 minutes

Wrapping Method

The Crescent
→ Page 15

Cooking Method
**"Flower Blossom"
Pan Frying**
→ Page 24

MATERIALS
[makes 12]

12 gyoza wrappers
1½ cups (250 g) minced lamb
1 teaspoon ground coriander
2 teaspoons cumin seeds
Fresh coriander leaves, for garnish

Top-Shelf Shrimp Dumplings

Sometimes we just need something warm and soft to sit down to, something to soothe aching muscles or perhaps an aching heart. The addition of *uni* sea-urchin roe to these simmered shrimp dumplings takes them out of the realm of the ordinary. They can be served in a soup or as a juicy side dish, but be careful not to overcook! The wrapping will fall apart if it's cooked too long.

Serves
6

Prep Time
45 minutes, plus time to make the Meat & Vegetable Filling

Wrapping Method

Santa's Gift Bag
→ Page 17

Cooking Method
Simmering
→ Page 24

MATERIALS
[makes 12]

12 gyoza wrappers
12 small raw shrimp (spot prawns or gulf shrimp)
4 tablespoons uni sea-urchin roe
4 tablespoons Meat & Vegetable Filling (page 12)

Cook the dumplings al dente—no longer than a minute and a half—so they don't get too soft.

TIP!
Look for uni sea-urchin roe in the sushi section of a large Asian grocer (it may also be found frozen). It will not keep for more than a day, so purchase only as much as you can use immediately. If you can't find uni, substitute caviar for an equally top-shelf experience.

TIP!
Be sure not to overcook these, or the wrapper will fall apart. A minute and a half of steaming should suffice.

"Santa Clam" Gyoza

Want to get festive for the holiday season? These "Santa Clam" dumplings will decorate your plate and your party to bring a festive air to any occasion. The addition of shrimp and a bit of cod meat makes for a jolly combination of flavors and textures. Close and seal the dumpling tightly around the tip of the clam to make Santa's "hat." Surf clams may be found in the freezer section of your local Asian market.

07

Serves
4

Prep Time
50 minutes

Wrapping Method

The Crescent
→ Page 15

Cooking Method
Steaming
→ Page 24

HOHOHO~

MATERIALS
[makes 8]

8 gyoza wrappers (use large size if available)
8 small surf clams
8 small fresh shrimp
1½ oz (35 g) white cod meat

Ho, Ho, Ho! Take the opportunity to use a common sashimi ingredient, the surf clam (also called "ark shell"), in this unusual dumpling!

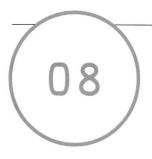

Bacon & Egg Carbonara Potstickers

The union of dumpling and Italian-style carbonara is almost too perfect. Carbonara, which originated in Rome, is a pasta dish composed of egg, hard cheese, bacon, and pepper. Whether you use thinly sliced and peppered Italian bacon, thick and juicy Canadian bacon, or smoky American bacon is up to you. Just be ready for the cooking aroma to draw a crowd of hungry family members.

Serves
4

Prep Time
**45 minutes, plus time
to make the sauce**

Wrapping Method

The Crescent
→ Page 15

Cooking Method
Pan Frying
→ Page 23

MATERIALS
[makes 8]

8 gyoza wrappers (use large size if available)
4 eggs, separated
2 tablespoons chopped bacon
8 teaspoons freshly grated pecorino romano
or Parmesan cheese (optional)

Egg Yolk Dumpling Sauce (Prep time: 15 mins)

½ cup (100 g) clarified butter
4 egg yolks
½ teaspoon salt
1 clove garlic, finely minced

In a small pan over a low flame, heat the clarified butter until it starts to bubble. Meanwhile, beat the egg yolks and salt together in a glass or ceramic bowl.

When the butter is hot, add the garlic and stir for 30 seconds. Add the garlic butter to the egg yolks 1 tablespoon at a time, whisking constantly, until all the butter has been incorporated. This must be done gradually, or the sauce will curdle! The sauce should thicken and become glossy as the butter is whisked in. Drizzle over the gyoza while hot.

Separate the eggs and lightly scramble the whites for the dumpling filling—don't cook them fully. Use the yolks to make a richly flavored sauce for the gyoza (see below). Add 1 teaspoon of cheese to each dumpling, if desired.

Place a heaping teaspoon of meat filling on a wrapper and top with a baby scallop and a pinch of fennel. Press down to remove any air, and wrap tightly.

Be-My-Baby Scallop Dumplings

Need something fancy to serve in a pinch? These scallop dumplings don't take much time to prepare, but using the shells for the presentation creates an impressive appetizer that'll make everybody want to be your baby! Be sure to scrub the shells clean before serving.

Serves
4

Prep Time
35 minutes, plus time to make the Chopped Meat Filling

Wrapping Method

The Crescent
→ Page 15

Cooking Method
Pan Frying
→ Page 23

MATERIALS
[makes 8]

8 gyoza wrappers
8 baby scallops
3 tablespoons Chopped Meat Filling (page 13)
2 teaspoons chopped fresh fennel, plus more for garnish

Fill with 2 scant teaspoons of sweet bean paste and an equal amount of fresh mozzarella. Sprinkle a thin layer of kinako powder on the serving plate and place the cooked dumplings on top.

10

Strawberry, Mozzarella & Sweet Bean Paste Dumplings

The use of *kinako* (roasted soybean flour) might have you dreaming of mochi—especially since these dumplings contain sweet bean paste, too. But strawberries mixed with mozzarella might give you pause. The two pair surprisingly well together. If you don't believe me, look up strawberry mozzarella salad—it's one of the most popular salads on earth. *Bocconcini* (fresh mozzarella shaped into small balls) are ideal for these gyoza, but any fresh mozzarella will work.

Sweet adzuki-bean paste (called *an* or *anko* in Japanese) can be found at most Asian markets—or you can make your own from cooked adzuki beans and granulated sugar. And if you can't track down kinako powder for your serving plate, substitute lightly toasted almond flour, roasted peanut powder, or toasted white sesame seeds.

MATERIALS
[makes 8]

8 gyoza wrappers (use large size if available)
8 small fresh strawberries
5 tablespoons sweet bean paste
½ cup (50 g) fresh mozzarella
Kinako roasted-soybean powder, as desired

Serves
4

Prep Time
30 minutes

Wrapping Method

The Volcano
→ Page 19

Cooking Method
Pan Frying
→ Page 23

Once the gyoza are cooked and arranged on a serving plate,
alternately top with uni sea urchin or salmon roe from the fridge.

Red Hot & Cool Volcano Gyoza

Let's face it: variety can take too much time. The Volcano wrapping method is a great solution to this problem—stuff the dumplings with a versatile and satisfying filling, then top them with ingredients that offer a flavor and temperature contrast. *Uni* sea urchin and salmon roe are just the starting point for toppings. With imagination and an adventurous palate, there's no limit to what you can do.

MATERIALS
[makes 8]

8 gyoza wrappers
8 small shrimp
4 oz (110 g) white-fleshed fish such as cod, halibut, flounder or tilapia, cubed
4 teaspoons sea urchin roe (for topping)
4 teaspoons salmon roe (for topping)

Serves
4

Prep Time
40 minutes

Wrapping Method

The Volcano
→ Page 19

Cooking Method
Pan Frying
→ Page 23

🎈 **TIP!**

Enjoy the hot and cold contrast of these dumplings!

Ooh La La Dumplings

Green cabbage has a strong flavor that mellows as it cooks. Napa cabbage tends to be milder and sweeter, but it gets soggy with cooking. Equal parts of both, with *ami* dried baby shrimp for depth of flavor, balance these dumplings to make a perfect treat. Toss some glutinous rice flour (*kyorikiko*) into the pan to get a lacy, crispy surface on the base of your dumplings. Kyorikiko is available in Asian markets. If you can't track it down, substitute cornstarch or potato starch. Ami dried baby shrimp can be found in Asian markets as well. If you can't find them, chopped ham will do.

Serves
4

Prep Time
30 minutes

Wrapping Method

The Crescent
→ Page 15

Cooking Method
**"Flower Blossom"
Pan Frying**
→ Page 24

**MATERIALS
[makes 8]**

8 gyoza wrappers
½ cup (50 g) green cabbage, chopped fine
½ cup (50 g) napa cabbage, chopped fine
3 tablespoons ami dried baby shrimp
¼ teaspoon salt

Too much of either type of cabbage will throw the flavor and texture out of balance. Aim for a perfect 1:1 ratio. Combine all ingredients and let stand a few minutes before filling your gyoza.

Blanch the sprouts and wrap them while still hot. Pull the sprouts up to make them stick out of the dumpling.

What's-Up Dumplings

A forest on your plate! These dumplings are another way to change "boring" side-dish vegetables into a fun set piece. Aralia sprouts, known as "the devil's walking stick" in Japan, grow in big, thorny thickets near the forest's edge. But they're packed with fiber and vitamins to help your health take root. If you can't find them, try using stalks of asparagus, broccoli raab or fiddlehead ferns.

Serves
4

Prep Time
**35 minutes, plus time
to make the Meat &
Vegetable Filling**

Wrapping Method

The Volcano
→ Page 19

Cooking Method
Pan Frying
→ Page 23

MATERIALS
[makes 8]

8 gyoza wrappers
8 aralia sprouts
½ cup (110 g) Meat & Vegetable Filling (page 12)

14

"Cheeseburger" Dumplings

Do you have a bit of hamburger left in the fridge, but not enough for burgers all around? Cheeseburger gyoza to the rescue! These dumplings are easily adapted to go with any main course. As part of a Mexican buffet, use Queso or Oaxaca cheese with a salsa verde dipping sauce. To pair with brisket, switch to Monterey Jack cheese and dip them in barbecue sauce. The possibilities really are endless. For a bold, all-American flavor, use sharp cheddar. For a subtler bite, use provolone or Parmesan. Want to make the cheese the centerpiece? Try Emmental or Gruyère. Sprinkling the cheese over the dumplings when the steaming step of pan-frying is almost done makes for a crispy, flavorful bottom layer and leaves space for more meat inside.

MATERIALS
[makes 8]

8 gyoza wrappers (use large size if available)
½ cup (110 g) Chopped Meat Filling (page 13) or leftover hamburger
1 cup (110 g) shredded cheese
8 leaves fresh basil, for garnish

Serves
4

Prep Time
25 minutes

Wrapping Method

The Crescent
→ Page 15

Cooking Method
Pan Frying
→ Page 23

Experiment with a variety of cheeses to create different flavors.

TIP!

Once plated, garnish with the basil leaves.

TIP!

Sprinkle cheese on the dumplings after you remove the lid at the end of cooking, and then cover for one more minute before turning off the heat.

Pinch the gyoza skin around the mushroom stem and wrap tightly. Alternately, you can cut the stem shorter and simply insert the mushroom into the cavity at the top of the wrapped dumpling.

Beech Mushroom and Pork Dumplings

15

Shimeji (beech mushrooms) are native to East Asia, where they're often found growing on beech trees. Both the mushroom cap and the stem are edible, but they should be cooked first to get rid of their naturally bitter taste. After cooking, they impart a nutty flavor with a slight crunch. If you can't find beech mushrooms at the market, substitute quartered baby bella or button mushrooms. These dumplings are fun to make, and they look right at home on a wooden serving tray.

Serves
5

Prep Time
35 minutes, plus time to make the Chopped Meat Filling

Wrapping Method

The Volcano
→ Page 19

Cooking Method
Pan Frying
→ Page 23

MATERIALS
[makes 10]

10 gyoza wrappers
¾ cup (150 g) Chopped Meat Filling (page 13)
10 beech mushrooms

You'll want to keep extras in the fridge for a future side dish. These dumplings are addictive!

Garlic Scape Dumplings with Beef

We all know garlic is good in almost anything. But pair juicy garlic scapes with tender cuts of beef and you'll be transported to another dimension. If your dreams are more to the tune of steak tartare than Venetian cuisine, try dipping this dumpling in Worcestershire sauce—it'll make you see stars!

Look for garlic scapes at your local farmers' market in spring—they are the plump, curly center shoots that emerge as the garlic matures. If you can't find them, you can use the lower part of green onions (scallions) instead, and squeeze a clove of garlic over the beef.

16

Serves
4

Prep Time
40 minutes

Wrapping Method

The Crescent
→ Page 15

Cooking Method
**"Flower Blossom"
Pan Frying**
→ Page 24

MATERIALS
[makes 8]

8 gyoza wrappers
Six 1½-inch (3-cm) lengths garlic scapes
4 oz (110 g) beef flank steak, slivered

17

Pork Dumplings with Shiso

Shiso, a perennial of the mint family, is sometimes called "beefsteak plant" or Japanese basil in the US. It's used as an accent in a variety of dishes, including noodles, tofu and sashimi. It's especially handy because it works not just as a beautiful base for any plated dish, but also as a wrapper. It's often served under sashimi, for example, so you can fold it around a morsel, dip it in soy sauce, and eat both together without getting your hands all fishy. It's also pretty hardy, so if you come across shiso seeds, you can try growing your own.

Serves
4

Prep Time
15 minutes, plus time to make the Chopped Meat Filling

Wrapping Method

The Crescent
→ Page 15

Cooking Method
"Flower Blossom" Pan Frying
→ Page 24

MATERIALS
[makes 8]

8 gyoza wrappers (use large size if available)
¾ cup (150 g) Chopped Meat Filling (page 13)
8 shiso leaves

One large shiso leaf serves as an inner wrapper for each dumpling.

58

Round out the flavor of each dumpling by placing a cherry tomato in the top!

TIP!
Brown the beef, then stir in the zucchini and tomato sauce to make the filling.

Gyoza Bolognese with Fresh Tomato

18

Bolognese sauce originated in the Italian city of Bologna during the eighteenth century. At first, it was a slightly nuanced take on *ragù*, a meat sauce that didn't even require tomato. When incorporated into ragù, the tomatoes served as a subtle flavoring for the meat, rather than being the main focus. As Bolognese evolved, the tomato came to dominate the sauce, balancing the heaviness of the meat. In this recipe we side with Bolognese over ragù, topping each dumpling with tomato for a lighter finish.

Serves
7

Prep Time
45 minutes

Wrapping Method

The Volcano
→ Page 19

Cooking Method
Pan Frying
→ Page 23

MATERIALS
[makes 14]

14 gyoza wrappers (use large size if available)
5 oz (150 g) beef flank steak, chopped fine
¼ cup (35 g) chopped zucchini
3 tablespoons tomato sauce
14 cherry tomatoes
Parsley for garnish

19

Tofu Dumplings with Okra & Pickled Ginger

Shopping for okra can be a little tricky. Look for tender, bright-green pods that are firm but not tough—they should snap in half easily. Avoid pods that are curled, blemished, or overly dry. Note that okra goes bad in low temperatures, so don't store it below 45 degrees. Wait to rinse until just before using, since contact with water makes the pods slimy. Sliced fresh okra makes the perfect garnish for these flavorful dumplings.

Atsu-age—thickly sliced deep-fried tofu—is available in the refrigerated section of most Asian groceries. Don't confuse it with *abura-age*, deep-fried tofu skins! If you can't find atsu-age, slice a block of tofu horizontally into three slabs, wrap each slab in several layers of paper towel and press under a weighted cutting board for two hours to remove as much moisture as possible, then deep-fry until golden brown on both sides.

Serves
4

Prep Time
40 minutes, plus time to make sauce and atsu-age (if needed)

Wrapping Method

The Crescent
→ Page 15

Cooking Method
Steaming
→ Page 24

Materials
[makes 8]

8 gyoza wrappers (use large size if available)
5 oz (150 g) atsu-age deep-fried tofu
1 tablespoon shredded pickled ginger
1 pod fresh young okra
Sweet Sauce (see sidebar)

If you fall in love with this recipe, try adding more ginger for an even bigger punch.

Sweet Sauce (Prep time: 10 minutes)

In a small saucepan, combine:

    2 tablespoons soy sauce
    6 tablespoons dashi stock or water
    2 tablespoons mirin
    2 teaspoons cornstarch
    2 teaspoons brown sugar

Whisk to blend, then place over medium-low heat and bring to a simmer, stirring frequently, until the sauce thickens.

TIP!
Pour the sauce over steamed dumplings and sprinkle with the okra slices.

Grab a couple mangoes next time they're half price at the super-market, and get a few bananas too. You'll be in for a treat!

Fried Banana & Mango Dumplings

Banana and mango make for a sweet and creamy treat—in fact, this fried dumpling may remind you of Mexican fried ice cream. Bananas grow in Latin America, the Caribbean—and even in Miyazaki, Japan. India is responsible for almost half of the world's mangoes, and China produces most of the gyoza wrappers. Just think—the ingredients on your plate have traveled around the planet to reach you, culminating in one delicious dish.

20

MATERIALS
[makes 8]

8 gyoza wrappers (use large size if available)
2 small bananas, peeled and chopped
1 mango, peeled and chopped
Blueberries for garnish

Serves
4

Prep Time
30 minutes

Wrapping Method

The Crescent
→ Page 15

Cooking Method
Deep Frying
→ Page 24

Cut a 3 to 4-inch (8 to 10-cm) piece from the end of each tentacle. Finely chop the rest of the octopus and use a heaping teaspoon as filling for each dumpling.

TIP!
For a memorable presentation, serve the dumplings in the frying pan, so it looks like the dancing legs are barely restrained by the pan.

Dancing Octopus Dumplings

Add a little adventure to your kitchen! When it comes to inventive ingredients, octopus is king. It adds a shock of color to your meal, as well as visual appeal with its curly tentacles and pretty round suckers. Properly prepared, it is tender and flavorful.

It's best to simmer the octopus the day before so that it will have time to cool down slowly and tenderize. Using frozen octopus is recommended, rather than buying fresh, since the freezing and thawing can help soften the meat. Larger Asian markets and specialty food stores often carry whole frozen octopus. For this dish, use two small (less than ½ pound, or 250 g) octopuses instead of one larger one, so you have lots of legs for the presentation.

21

Serves
8

Prep Time
45 minutes, plus time to make Simmered Octopus

Wrapping Method

The Seashell
→ Page 20

Cooking Method
Pan Frying
→ Page 23

**MATERIALS
[makes 16]**

16 gyoza wrappers (use large size if available)
2 small octopuses, simmered (see sidebar)

Simmered Octopus (Prep time: 30 mins, plus 4 to 12 hours cooling time)

2 small frozen octopuses (about 1 lb / 500 g total)
4 tablespoons salt, divided
4-in (10-cm) length kombu seaweed
½ daikon radish, grated

Place the frozen octopus in cool water for about an hour to thaw. In a large pan or stockpot, combine about a gallon (4 liters) of cold water with the kombu kelp and 3 tablespoons of the sea salt and bring to a boil. Meanwhile, cut out the beaks (on the underside of the octopus, where the legs come together) and either remove and discard the heads or cut open and invert to remove the ink sac and viscera. Combine the grated daikon with the remaining 1 tablespoon salt and rub all over the octopuses to clean them.

When the water comes to a boil, hold each octopus with tongs and dip into the boiling water a few times until the legs curl up. Reduce heat to a bare simmer, place the octopuses in the water and simmer uncovered for 5 minutes. Remove from heat, cover, and allow to cool for an hour, then transfer the pot to the refrigerator and allow to cool at least 4 hours more (overnight is best). Trim the tough skin from around the head and the base of the legs, then cut as desired.

Kelp & Clam Gyoza

Kobashira, a sushi specialty, is the adductor muscle of the surf clam. Valued for their texture and complexity of flavor, these dainty morsels can be found at a large Japanese market where sushi-grade seafood is sold. They may also be found in the freezer section. If you can't find them, substitute surf clams themselves for a similar full-on marine flavor.

Kombu kelp is most often found dried. Soak in cold water until soft (30 minutes to an hour) before chopping finely. Use any extra kombu for a refreshing garnish.

Serves
4

Prep Time
40 minutes

Wrapping Method

The Volcano
→ Page 19

Cooking Method
Pan Frying
→ Page 23

MATERIALS
[makes 8]

8 gyoza wrappers
3½ oz (85 g) fresh or reconstituted kombu kelp, minced
3½ oz (85 g) kobashira or clam meat, chopped

Go ahead and make a heap of these yummy dumplings!

TIP!
If you like wasabi, throw some in. Finish it off by topping each dumpling with more clams!

You can substitute zucchini, greens or green beans for the bell peppers. Sauté in a little olive oil or butter and seasoning, then add the beaten eggs. Don't cook the eggs all the way, though; they'll reach perfection as the dumplings are steamed.

Bell Pepper Dumplings with Egg

This egg and veggie dumpling can be a great breakfast on the run—or you can make a quick lunch or dinner out of the leftovers of your morning omelet. Placed on a bed of fennel, they look like pale bird eggs in a nest out of Dr. Seuss.

MATERIALS
[makes 8]

8 gyoza wrappers
½ cup (50 g) thinly sliced bell pepper
2 eggs, beaten
Fennel fronds or other greens,
for serving

Serves
4

Prep Time
30 minutes

Wrapping Method

The Sailor Cap
→ Page 18

Cooking Method
Pan Frying
→ Page 23

Shiitake & Pork Potstickers

Shiitake mushrooms have a meaty flavor all on their own, but they explode with flavor when combined with real meat, adding a rich taste to rival that top layer of buttery dough. We recommend fresh shiitakes in this recipe, but if you'd like a chewier texture and an earthier flavor, use an equivalent amount of reconstituted dried mushrooms. For instructions on how to reconstitute dried shiitakes, see page 9.

MATERIALS
[makes 12]

12 gyoza wrappers
½ cup (110 g) Meat & Vegetable Filling (page 12)
1 cup (180 g) finely chopped shiitake mushrooms
Garlic Chips (see sidebar) for garnish

Serves
6

Prep Time
35 minutes, plus time to make the Meat & Vegetable Filling and the Garlic Chips

Wrapping Method

The Crescent
→ Page 15

Cooking Method
"Flower Blossom"
Pan Frying
→ Page 24

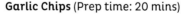

Garlic Chips (Prep time: 20 mins)

Place 1 cup peanut or canola oil in a wok or heavy-bottomed pan and bring to 350°F (175°C). Add ¼ cup (40 g, about 12 cloves) thinly sliced garlic in a single layer and cook, stirring and tossing, for 1 to 2 minutes, until just golden brown. Use a slotted spoon to transfer to a plate covered with several layers of paper towel and allow to drain and cool. Store in a tightly covered container. Keeps for a week. (Tip: Use the same oil and method to make crispy fried shallots, then save the oil for seasoning or salad dressing!)

You can use reconstituted dried shiitake mushrooms if you prefer, but it will change the texture.

> **TIP!**
> Mix the chopped fresh basil with the olive oil and drizzle over these dumplings for an exquisite finish.

This Chinese-influenced ingredient—*butaniku no kakuni*, or simmered pork belly—is an incredible match for the springy, moist dough of a dumpling.

Simmered Pork Belly Dumplings

Pork belly is a delicacy across the world, and anyone can see why—this boneless, fatty cut of meat adds depth of flavor to dishes with rich seasonings and tangy sauces. Use only the best cuts of pork belly to make your dumplings stand out.

Serves
4

Prep Time
30 minutes, plus time to make the Simmered Pork Belly

Wrapping Method

The Seashell
→ Page 20

Cooking Method
Pan Frying
→ Page 23

MATERIALS
[makes 8]

8 gyoza wrappers
5 oz (150 g) Simmered Pork Belly (see sidebar), chopped fine
2 tablespoons extra-virgin olive oil, for sauce
1 tablespoon chopped fresh basil, for sauce

Simmered Pork Belly (Prep time: 3 hours)

1 lb (500 g) pork belly, cut into 2-by-6-inch (5-x-15-cm) lengths
2 green onions (scallions), trimmed, white parts only
1 oz (30 g) fresh ginger root, peeled and sliced thickly
3 tablespoons dark soy sauce
7 tablespoons sake
7 tablespoons water
2 tablespoons brown sugar

Place the pork, green onions and ginger in a large pot and cover with fresh water. Bring to a boil over high heat, then turn heat to low and simmer for 2 hours (use a drop lid if you have one; alternately, cut a round of parchment with a slit in the center to rest directly on the simmering pork). Add water if needed to keep the pork covered. Use tongs to remove the pork carefully (it will break easily) and rinse in cold water. Combine the soy sauce, sake, water and brown sugar in a saucepan and stir to dissolve the sugar. Add the rinsed pork and bring to a boil, then cover with a drop lid (or parchment with a slit cut in it, as above) and cook, shaking occasionally to coat the meat, for 25 minutes, or until the sauce is reduced to 2 or 3 tablespoons. Remove from heat and serve. If using in dumplings, allow to cool before filling the gyoza skins.

The "Colonel's" Crispy Chicken Dumplings

The crisp fried chicken inside a tender dumpling skin will give your family a tasty surprise! Great for football parties or as an easy appetizer or side dish, these fried chicken dumplings are a snap to make. You can fry the chicken yourself or get takeout—we won't tell!

MATERIALS
[makes 8]

8 large gyoza wrappers (use large size if available)
5 oz (150 g) fried chicken pieces, bones removed
Lemon wedges for garnish

Serves
4

Prep Time
30 minutes

Wrapping Method

The Crescent
→ Page 15

Cooking Method
Deep Frying
→ Page 24

The crunchiness of the filling will vary depending on how finely the fried chicken is chopped—if you like it crunchier, leave the chicken pieces larger.

TIP!
Fry at 365°F (180°C) until the dumplings turn golden brown.

Cook and eat these dumplings without delay after wrapping so the filling maintains its textural contrast.

Radish & Shredded Squid Dumplings

Did you know that daikon radishes are packed with potassium, which relaxes blood vessels, both reducing blood pressure and increasing blood flow throughout the body? And squid meat contains compounds known to lower the chance of stroke or heart attack. So these hearty dumplings not only taste good, but are good for you! *Saki ika* semi-dried seasoned squid can be found in the snack-food section of your local Asian market—or order it online.

27

Serves
4

Prep Time
30 minutes, plus time to make the Simmered Daikon Radish

Wrapping Method

The Crescent
→ Page 15

Cooking Method
Pan Frying
→ Page 23

**MATERIALS
[makes 8]**

8 gyoza wrappers
½ cup (100 g) coarsely chopped simmered daikon radish (see sidebar)
1 oz (30 g) *saki ika* seasoned dried squid, cut into ½ inch (1 cm) lengths

---

Simmered Daikon Radish (Prep time: 2½ hours)

4 cups (1 liter) dashi stock or water
1 x 2-in (3 x 5-cm) piece dried kombu kelp
1 tablespoon sake
2 teaspoons sugar
1 teaspoon salt
2 tablespoons soy sauce
1 lb (500 g) daikon radish, peeled and cut into 1-in (2.5-cm) rounds
2 tablespoons mirin

In a medium saucepan over medium heat, combine the dashi, kombu, sake, sugar, salt and soy sauce. Stir to combine. Bevel the edges of each daikon round and add to the liquid ingredients. Bring to a boil and let cook for 10 minutes, skimming off any foam, then lower the heat to a simmer and allow to cook for about 2 hours more, until tender. Stir in the mirin at the end, remove from heat, and allow to cool slowly.

Crunchy Land Seaweed Gyoza

Land seaweed or saltwort (*Salsola komarovii*, called *okahijiki* in Japanese) is a unique plant that grows in saline marshes and other areas where the soil is high in salt. It is a succulent with a crunchy texture and a unique salt-and-pepper flavor. You can find it growing wild in coastal areas and, more rarely, in Asian markets. Though the texture isn't the same, arugula is an acceptable substitute with a similar flavor profile.

28

Serves
6

Prep Time
**40 minutes, plus time
to make the Meat &
Vegetable Filling**

Wrapping Method

The Crescent
→ Page 15

Cooking Method
**"Flower Blossom"
Pan Frying**
→ Page 24

**MATERIALS
[makes 12]**

12 gyoza wrappers
4 oz (110 g) land seaweed, roughly chopped
¾ cup (150 g) Meat & Vegetable Filling (page 12)

Even when it's chopped and cooked, land seaweed maintains its crispness. Enjoy the extra crunch in your gyoza!

Maybe these gyoza will herald the dawn of a new era where land seaweed rules!

Corned Beef & Shallot Potstickers

29

Corned beef gets its name from the salt "corns," the large rock crystals used to preserve the meat so that it will last for months. While it crested in popularity during the food rationing of World War I and World War II, it remains a longstanding comfort food for many, especially in the iconic pairing of corned beef and cabbage. Combining corned beef with shallots makes for a lighter, more vibrant taste that is enhanced by your favorite dipping sauce.

Serves
6

Prep Time
40 minutes

Wrapping Method

The Crescent
→ Page 15

Cooking Method
Pan Frying
→ Page 23

MATERIALS
[makes 12]

12 gyoza wrappers
4 oz (110 g) corned beef
3 shallots, chopped finely
Dried vegetables, for garnish

Use the entire shallot—even the purple part—cut up fine.

TIP!
In summer,
try throwing
these on the grill.

If your sweet potatoes aren't very sweet,
add a little brown sugar.

Sweet Potato Dumplings

30

Sweet potatoes are such a great staple—they keep a long time; they're packed with nutrients; and they're versatile enough to use in soups, salads, tempura, main dishes—and now, dumplings! The sweet-potato filling goes perfectly with the chewy wrapper, especially when dipped in soy sauce.

MATERIALS
[makes 8]

8 gyoza wrappers (use large size if available)
1 large baked sweet potato, peeled and mashed (see sidebar)
Brown sugar and soy sauce to taste

Serves
4

Prep Time
20 minutes, plus time to bake the sweet potato

Wrapping Method

The Crescent
→ Page 15

Cooking Method
Broiling
→ Page 24

Baked Sweet Potato (Prep time: 50 minutes)

Heat the oven to 400°F (200°C). Pierce the sweet potato in several locations with a fork. Place the sweet potato on a rimmed baking sheet lined with foil. Bake until tender, about 45 minutes.

Sauté the abalone in butter and toss with soy sauce, then wrap.

Buttery Abalone Gyoza

These simple, seductive dumplings are a buttery classic. Sauté the abalone slowly, so it has time to fully absorb the butter before stuffing. Once served, keep a sharp eye on your diners, as they tend to suffer from "empty plate" syndrome.

Abalone is widely available frozen, especially at Asian markets. Wild-caught abalone is quite expensive, so opt for the smaller farmed steaks. If you can't find abalone, substitute clams or scungilli.

31

Serves
4

Prep Time
35 minutes

Wrapping Method

The Crescent
→ Page 15

Cooking Method
Pan Frying
→ Page 23

MATERIALS
[makes 8]

8 gyoza wrappers
2 small (2 oz / 50 g each) abalone steaks,
roughly chopped
2 tablespoons butter
2 teaspoons soy sauce, or to taste

So many vegetable leaves have their own unique flavors;
we've got to try them all!

Angelic Ashitaba Dumplings

Ashitaba (meaning "tomorrow leaf," so named because its leaves grow back overnight when cut) is a Japanese variety of angelica, a bright green herb in the carrot family. Like Western angelica, it has a fresh, slightly bitter flavor, and is highly valued for its health benefits. It may be a challenge to find ashitaba even at a well-stocked Asian market. If you're lucky enough to have access to fresh young angelica leaves, you can use those; otherwise try using lovage leaves, celery leaves, or even flat-leafed Italian parsley as a substitute. These dumplings go beautifully with a glass of merlot.

Serves
4

Prep Time
**30 minutes, plus time
to make the Meat &
Vegetable Filling**

Wrapping Method

The Penguin
→ Page 21

Cooking Method
Pan Frying
→ Page 23

MATERIALS
[makes 8]

8 gyoza wrappers
½ cup (30 g) roughly chopped fresh ashitaba
½ cup (110 g) Meat & Vegetable Filling (page 12)

Okra & Nameko Mushroom Gyoza

Nameko mushrooms are small, orange-capped fungi with a sweet, mild flavor and a pleasant crunch. They are available at Asian grocery stores fresh in winter months and in cans or jars at other times of the year.

Be sure to chop the okra finely for a consistent base that will help anchor the slippery mushrooms. A garnish of watercress or baby arugula will add a pleasant bite to these soft gyoza.

MATERIALS
[makes 8]

8 gyoza wrappers (use large size if available)
15 pods fresh okra, minced
3 oz (75 g) fresh or drained canned nameko mushrooms
Watercress or baby arugula for garnish

Serves
4

Prep Time
30 minutes

Wrapping Method

The Crescent
→ Page 15

Cooking Method
Pan Frying
→ Page 23

🎈 TIP!
These gyoza are easier to wrap if you enclose the mushrooms fully.

Try other wrapping techniques to see which you like best!

Rinse the konnyaku in cold water, drain well, chop and sauté in a little sesame oil.

Squid Ink, Konnyaku & Anchovy Gyoza

Squid ink, sometimes called "the flavor of the ocean," lends a captivating silky, briny flavor to any dish. The intriguing color of squid ink, combined with the unique texture of the *konnyaku* and the umami bomb of the anchovy, deepens the taste of these dumplings. The *ami* shrimp lighten the intensity. You can find squid ink at your local fish market, or at Italian or Spanish specialty shops—just look for small black packets or jars.

Konnyaku, made from devil's-tongue root, comes in cake or noodle form; use the noodles (*shirataki*) for this recipe. You can find them in any Asian market or in a large grocery store, usually in the same area as tofu, miso, tempeh and wonton wrappers.

Serves
4

Prep Time
45 minutes, plus time to deep-fry garlic

Wrapping Method

The Crescent
→ Page 15

Cooking Method
Pan Frying
→ Page 23

Top the filling with an anchovy and wrap.

MATERIALS
[makes 8]

8 gyoza wrappers
3 oz (75 g) konnyaku (shirataki) noodles, chopped and sautéed
2 packets (2 teaspoons) squid ink
1 tablespoon dried ami shrimp, or to taste
8 small anchovies
Whole deep-fried garlic cloves, for serving

Lotus Root & Pork Belly Potstickers

If you've got a hankering for a hot-pot dish like *sukiyaki*, *shabu-shabu*, or wonton soup, these dumplings will hit the spot and leave you feeling warm and satisfied. Lotus root can be purchased in fresh form, or presliced in vacuum-packed bags. If using fresh roots, peel, cut in half crosswise, and wash the interior thoroughly before slicing. Slice the whole root and store the leftovers in water to prevent browning.

Serves
4

Prep Time
35 minutes

Wrapping Method

The Crescent
→ Page 15

Cooking Method
**"Flower Blossom"
Pan Frying**
→ Page 24

MATERIALS
[makes 8]

8 gyoza wrappers
3½ oz (85 g) sliced pork belly, chopped
8 thin rounds lotus root (about 3 oz / 80 g),
cut in halves or thirds as needed
1 small red chili, deseeded and sliced into thin
rings (optional)

Be sure the lotus root is sliced thinly.

TIP!
Fry the dumplings until they're well browned and crisp on the bottom.

Sweet Eel Dumplings

Though it's not quite as popular in the West, broiled eel is beloved in Asia for its mellow flavor and tender texture, enhanced by a richly flavored sauce. These dumplings are the perfect comfort food in good times and bad! Look for freshwater eel (*unagi*; broiled eel is *unagi kabayaki*) in the freezer section of your Asian grocer.

Serves
4

Prep Time
**30 minutes, plus time
to make the Sweet
Sauce**

Wrapping Method

The Crescent
→ Page 15

Cooking Method
Pan Frying
→ Page 23

MATERIALS
[makes 8]

8 gyoza wrappers
4 oz (110 g) cooked freshwater eel, sliced
Sweet Sauce (page 63), to taste

**Freshwater eel has a bolder taste than salt-water eel;
it tastes fantastic wrapped in a dumpling.**

Cheesy Chikuwa Gyoza

The warm aroma of melting cheese is reason enough to make these indulgent potstickers. *Chikuwa*, a type of grilled fish cake with a sweet, toasty flavor, can be found at an Asian market. Its tubular shape makes for pretty rings when you slice it. If you can't find chikuwa, *surimi* (artificial crab meat) is an acceptable substitute.

MATERIALS
[makes 8]

8 gyoza wrappers
2 oz (50 g) chikuwa, sliced (about two cakes)
¾ cup (75 g) shredded cheese (mild cheddar
or jack cheese work well)
Fresh-grated Parmesan cheese, for topping

Serves
4

Prep Time
30 minutes

Wrapping Method

The Crescent
→ Page 15

Cooking Method
**"Flower Blossom"
Pan Frying**
→ Page 24

 TIP!

**Sprinkle the Parmesan
over the gyoza, then broil.**

After pan-frying, sprinkle on Parmesan cheese and toss these under the broiler or in the toaster oven for an appealing browned finish.

Pollock Roe & Prawn Potstickers

The simple filling and easy-to-grab shape make this finger food a great addition to a party menu, especially with a variety of dipping sauces for your guests to try. Pair with a fruity white wine to really get the party started.

Tarako pollock roe may be found in the freezer section of your Asian grocery store. If you can't find it, Italian *bottarga* (salted mullet roe) would work as well. Wait until the last minute to cut the nori into thin strips, so the garnish stays crisp.

Serves
4

Prep Time
30 minutes

Wrapping Method

The Sailor Cap
→ Page 18

Cooking Method
Pan Frying
→ Page 23

MATERIALS
[makes 8]

8 gyoza wrappers
5 oz (150 g) fresh Gulf shrimp or spot prawns, chopped if necessary
2 tablespoons tarako pollock roe
½ sheet toasted sushi nori, cut into slivers, for garnish

Simply mix the shrimp with the pollock roe to fill. The texture and flavor of the slivered nori seaweed make it an indispensable topping.

Snappy Tuna Potstickers

The snap in these dumplings comes from sliced *myoga* ginger buds, which may be found in the produce section of a large Japanese or Asian market. Sliced ginger shoots or a tablespoon of very thinly sliced fresh ginger root can be used as a substitute.

A traditional sashimi garnish, *benitade* (ben-ee-tah-day) water-pepper sprouts make a nice bed for these potstickers. If you can't find them in the produce section of your local Asian market, substitute any kind of microgreens.

```
╭─────────────────────────────────────╮
            MATERIALS
            [makes 8]

         8 gyoza wrappers
   4 oz (110 g) well-drained canned tuna
3 myoga ginger buds, thinly sliced or shredded
   benitade sprouts or microgreens for serving
╰─────────────────────────────────────╯
```

Serves
4

Prep Time
30 minutes

Wrapping Method

The Crescent
→ Page 15

Cooking Method
**"Flower Blossom"
Pan Frying**
→ Page 24

> You can shred or chop the ginger bud according to your preference.

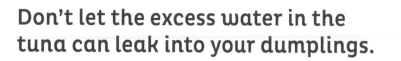

Don't let the excess water in the tuna can leak into your dumplings.

TIP!
Try different types of tuna, canned or fresh, to find your favorite combination for these gyoza.

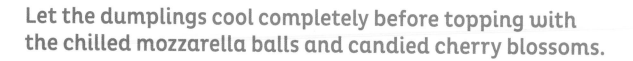

Let the dumplings cool completely before topping with
the chilled mozzarella balls and candied cherry blossoms.

Cherry Blossom Dumplings

The end of March is the best time to visit Japan if you want to see the cherry blossoms in bloom. It's a good time to make these dumplings, too, because the ingredients will be readily available. If it's too difficult to find white sweet bean paste (*shiro-an*) flavored with cherry blossoms, head to a Japanese bakery and pick up some sakura mochi—they'll be stuffed with it. Or just use regular *anko* (sweet adzuki-bean paste that can be found at most Asian markets).

40

Serves
5

Prep Time
40 minutes

Wrapping Method

The Volcano
→ Page 19

Cooking Method
Pan Frying
→ Page 23

MATERIALS
[makes 10]

10 gyoza wrappers (use large size if available)
½ cup (110 g) cherry-blossom-flavored white bean paste
10 candied cherry blossoms or other candied flowers
10 balls fresh mozzarella cheese

Peekaboo Squid Gyoza

Whether you're a novice or an expert in the kitchen, these easy-to-make baby squid dumplings are an impressive conversation starter around the dinner table. They can be plated on their own or served alongside other offerings as an accent piece. Just wrap and go!

MATERIALS
[makes 4]

4 gyoza wrappers (use large size if available)
4 baby squid, blanched in boiling water for 90 seconds,
then shocked in ice water and drained

Serves
4

Prep Time
20 minutes

Wrapping Method

The Crescent
→ Page 15

Cooking Method
Pan Frying
→ Page 23

Let the head and tentacles stick out from the sides of the wrapper!

Fish Sausage & Cucumber Dumplings

Fish sausage is healthier than red-meat sausages, as it is much more nutrient-dense. Combined with cucumber, it makes a filling bursting with flavor and textural complexity, taking these gyoza to the next level. Fair warning, though—these little packets are addictive.

If you can't find fish sausage at an Asian market, you can substitute *surimi*— or try hot dogs, if you like.

42

MATERIALS
[makes 8]

8 gyoza wrappers (use large size if available)
5 oz (150 g) fish sausage (about 3 sausages), coarsely chopped
1 oz (30 g) cucumber, cut into thin matchsticks

Serves
4

Prep Time
30 minutes

Wrapping Method

The Crescent
→ Page 15

Cooking Method
"Flower Blossom" Pan Frying
→ Page 24

Combined with the ground fish sausage, the fine-cut cucumber will give your gyoza a mouthwatering aroma.

43

Wagyu Beef Dumplings

These ingredients are perfection itself—you simply cannot go wrong with marbled Wagyu beef, cracked black pepper, and rosemary. The sauce is up to you. Whether it's *yakiniku*, barbecue sauce or A1, there's really no wrong answer. If you don't have access to Wagyu beef, use a marbled piece of sirloin; chill or freeze and slice thin.

MATERIALS
[makes 8]

8 gyoza wrappers
5 oz (150 g) Wagyu beef
Cracked black pepper to taste
Sauce of choice, for topping
4 sprigs rosemary, for garnish

Serves
4

Prep Time
25 minutes

Wrapping Method

The Crescent
→ Page 15

Cooking Method
"Flower Blossom"
Pan Frying
→ Page 24

A sprinkling of black pepper

Thinly sliced Wagyu beef

Wrap these dumplings tightly. You don't want a single succulent bite to escape.

TIP!
Fry at 365°F (180°C) until the dumplings turn golden-brown.

Once the dumplings are on the plate, add a slice of prosciutto on top!

Hold the natto in place with a small spoon to keep it from spilling out as you pinch the dumpling closed.

Natto & Prosciutto Dumplings

According to legend, a man living in northeastern Japan around 1000 CE placed warm cooked soybeans in a straw sack and saddled up for a long horseback journey. Upon opening the sack up quite a bit later, he discovered that he had made *natto*. A cultured food like tempeh or yogurt, natto is beloved by many, although some disparage it for its distinctive smell. If you can't obtain natto at your local Asian market (look in the freezer section), try crumbling up 5 ounces (150 g) of tempeh and sautéing it with a little soy sauce as a substitute.

Draping these deep-fried dumplings in prosciutto adds a captivating layer to the dish, while raisins counter the slight bitterness of the natto.

Wrapping the sticky natto beans can be tricky—have a damp cloth close at hand to wipe your fingers and utensils.

44

Serves
4

Prep Time
35 minutes

Wrapping Method

The Crescent
→ Page 15

Cooking Method
Deep Frying
→ Page 24

MATERIALS
[makes 8]

8 gyoza wrappers
3 tubs natto (one tub usually contains 1.6 oz / 50 g natto)
8 slices prosciutto
Raisins for garnish

Simmered Bamboo Shoot Gyoza

45

Just chop, cook, and eat! Slices of *naruto* fish cake will lend your dish a dash of color. Naruto may be recognized as an anime character in America, but the budding ninja's namesake is a type of *kamaboko* with a savory taste similar to lobster or crab. The pink swirl it bears is symbolic of the Naruto Whirlpools near Japan's Naruto Strait.

MATERIALS
[makes 8]

8 gyoza wrappers
5 oz (150 g) simmered bamboo shoots, sliced
8 slices naruto fish cake, for topping

Serves
4

Prep Time
30 minutes

Wrapping Method

The Crescent
→ Page 15

Cooking Method
"Flower Blossom"
Pan Frying
→ Page 24

Seasoned simmered bamboo shoots are available in cans or packages; all you have to do is slice and wrap.

Festive Red Rice Potstickers

In Japan, red rice (*sekihan*) is a festive dish served at the celebrations of life—the birth of a child, a coming-of-age ceremony, weddings, festivals, and of course New Year's! A filling dish that's both sweet and savory, red rice is composed of sweet rice mixed with red adzuki beans, which give the dish its signature color. While sekihan is usually served in bowls, I've crafted these red-rice gyoza to give your celebration one very memorable appetizer (with a lot less cleanup). You can make red rice for these delicious dumplings at home, or you can find it premade in the bento section of your local Japanese market. While you're there, see if you can find *gomashio* seasoning. If not, just mix 2 tablespoons black sesame seeds with ½ teaspoon of Himalayan salt.

MATERIALS
[makes 8]

8 gyoza wrappers
2 cups (400 g) sekihan red rice (see below)
Gomashio to taste

Serves
4

Prep Time
30 minutes, plus time to make the Festive Red Rice

Wrapping Method

The Crescent
→ Page 15

Cooking Method
Pan Frying
→ Page 23

Festive Red Rice (*Sekihan* — Serves 4; Prep time: 30 mins)

(*Note: be sure to reserve the cooking liquid from the beans; this is what will color the rice red.*)

½ cup (90 g) adzuki beans
1 cup (180 g) glutinous rice
½ cup (90 g) medium-grain white rice
¼ teaspoon salt
1 teaspoon sugar
⅛ teaspoon rice vinegar

Rinse the beans and bring to a boil in ample water over medium-high heat. Let boil for 3 minutes, then remove from heat and add cold water to cool to lukewarm. Drain, then return to the pot with 2½ cups (600 ml) water and bring to a boil. Reduce heat to a simmer and cook for 20 to 40 minutes, depending on age of beans, until they are firm but chewable. Remove from heat and drain, reserving the liquid. Allow both beans and liquid to cool.

While the beans are cooking, combine the two kinds of rice and rinse, drain, and let stand for 1 hour. Add enough water to the bean liquid to bring it to 2 cups (500 ml), then combine with the salt, sugar, and vinegar. Stir to blend, then add to rice cooker with the drained rice and beans. Cook on the regular setting.

You may need to take some of the rice out of the inarizushi so it can fit inside the gyoza wrapper.

This is another world first!

Fox-in-a-Blanket Gyoza

Wrap one of these gyoza in a shiso leaf for a refreshing surprise!

A dumpling within a dumpling! *Inarizushi*—named for Shinto deity Inari, the god of foxes, fertility, tea, sake and rice—is a fried tofu pocket stuffed with steamed rice, sometimes alongside other ingredients. Pick out your favorite inarizushi from the bento section of your local Asian market, wrap it together with a slice of pickled ginger, and enjoy a hot dumpling with some tea.

Serves
4

Prep Time
25 minutes

Wrapping Method

The Crescent
→ Page 15

Cooking Method
Pan Frying
→ Page 23

MATERIALS
[makes 8]

8 gyoza wrappers (use large size if available)
8 stuffed inarizushi pouches
8 slices pickled ginger
8 shiso leaves, for garnish

48

Takoyaki Gyoza

Everyone's favorite street treat, *takoyaki*—morsels of tender octopus covered in batter and fried into toothsome spheres—is the number one food tourists remember from their adventures in Japan. If you're lucky enough to live near a large Japanese market like Mitsuwa or Uwajimaya, you can find takoyaki in the bento area. Unfortunately, you need a special takoyaki griddle to make them yourself.

Adding an extra doughy layer to each takoyaki ball makes these gyoza extra satisfying. Just don't forget the takoyaki sauce at the end! The bonito flakes and aonori seaweed sprinkle are optional. All three can be found at the Asian grocery where you purchased your takoyaki, though. You can also whip up your own takoyaki sauce by mixing 3 tablespoons ketchup with 1 tablespoon Worcestershire sauce, 2 teaspoons soy sauce and 1 teaspoon of caster sugar or honey.

Serves
4

Prep Time
25 minutes

Wrapping Method

The Crescent
→ Page 15

Cooking Method
Pan Frying
→ Page 23

MATERIALS
[makes 8]

8 gyoza wrappers (use large size if available)
8 takoyaki balls
Takoyaki sauce to taste
Aonori seaweed flakes, to taste (optional)
katsuobushi dried bonito flakes, to taste (optional)

If you end up with extra takoyaki gyoza, try to polish it off immediately—reheating these dumplings is not recommended.

TIP!
Fry in 375°F (190°C) oil until the dumplings turn medium brown.

The Gyoza King highly recommends this one! Cook up one recipe of gyoza, then wrap each dumpling in a second gyoza skin and deep fry it for a dumpling that's exponentially delicious!

The Gyoza King's Double Deep Fried Dumplings

(49)

You read that right. Take your favorite dumpling recipe from this book, wrap it in another gyoza wrapper, and deep fry it! That's how you make the Gyoza King's Double Deep Fried Dumplings. As Elvis (another king) might tell you, deep-frying makes everything better.

MATERIALS
[makes 8]

8 gyoza wrappers (use large size if available)
8 prepared dumplings (any kind)

Serves
4

Prep Time
**Varies, depending on
the gyoza used**

Wrapping Method

The Crescent
→ Page 15

Cooking Method
Deep Frying
→ Page 24

We finally arrive at the last of my favorite dumplings. This one cuts straight to the heart of every gyoza recipe: it's pure gyoza, nothing else.

This gyoza is satisfying to master, but surprisingly difficult to make.

Light-as-a-Feather Puff Dumpling

Frying an empty gyoza skin is the pinnacle of gyoza achievement. This dumpling is all about the sauce! If you master the technique (which will be a challenge), it's a great way to use up gyoza wrappers or add an easy finishing touch to a meal that's already very heavy. Or turn them into dessert by sprinkling with powdered sugar and dipping in jam or chocolate syrup. The only limit is your imagination!

MATERIALS
[makes 1]

1 gyoza wrapper

Serves
1 (easily multiplied as needed)

Prep Time
5 minutes

Wrapping Method

The Crescent
→ Page 15

Cooking Method
Pan Frying
→ Page 23

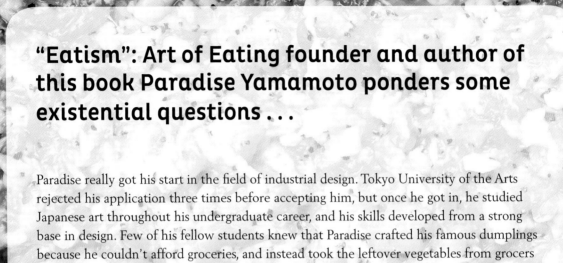

"Eatism": Art of Eating founder and author of this book Paradise Yamamoto ponders some existential questions . . .

Paradise really got his start in the field of industrial design. Tokyo University of the Arts rejected his application three times before accepting him, but once he got in, he studied Japanese art throughout his undergraduate career, and his skills developed from a strong base in design. Few of his fellow students knew that Paradise crafted his famous dumplings because he couldn't afford groceries, and instead took the leftover vegetables from grocers at the end of each day, making them into dumplings to give them some variety and taste.

For a brief period, he was captivated by painting, Latin music and railroads. His mind was open to everything the art world had to offer, nurtured by his quest to absorb every aspect of Western and Japanese art. From the Western world he studied Romanesque, Gothic, Renaissance, Baroque, Rococo and Impressionist art, as well as Belle Époque works, Cubism, Surrealism, Fauvism, metaphysical painting, Dadaism and more. From Japan, he examined Asuka culture, Nara culture, Higashiyama culture, Northern and Southern styles, the Kan School and rogue styles. His areas of interest were vast and ever-changing. He absorbed a wide range of artistic sensibilities by exploring myriad periods and styles. This book reveals his reasons for learning so much and studying so many art forms: the dumplings he cooks, their structural aesthetic, their particular taste are all expressions of his art. His art comes before his food; some may consider his dumplings avant-garde.

With this book as the starting point, the future of gyoza will not be limited to an inevitable series of thoughtless imitations coming one after the other until the gyoza tradition collapses under its own weight; instead, it will embrace the launch of the avant-garde gyoza.